BALLOON PUBLISHING

COLOR TEST PAGE

God is within her
She will not fail

Psalm 46:3

WE LOVE BECAUSE HE FIRST loved us

1 John 4:19

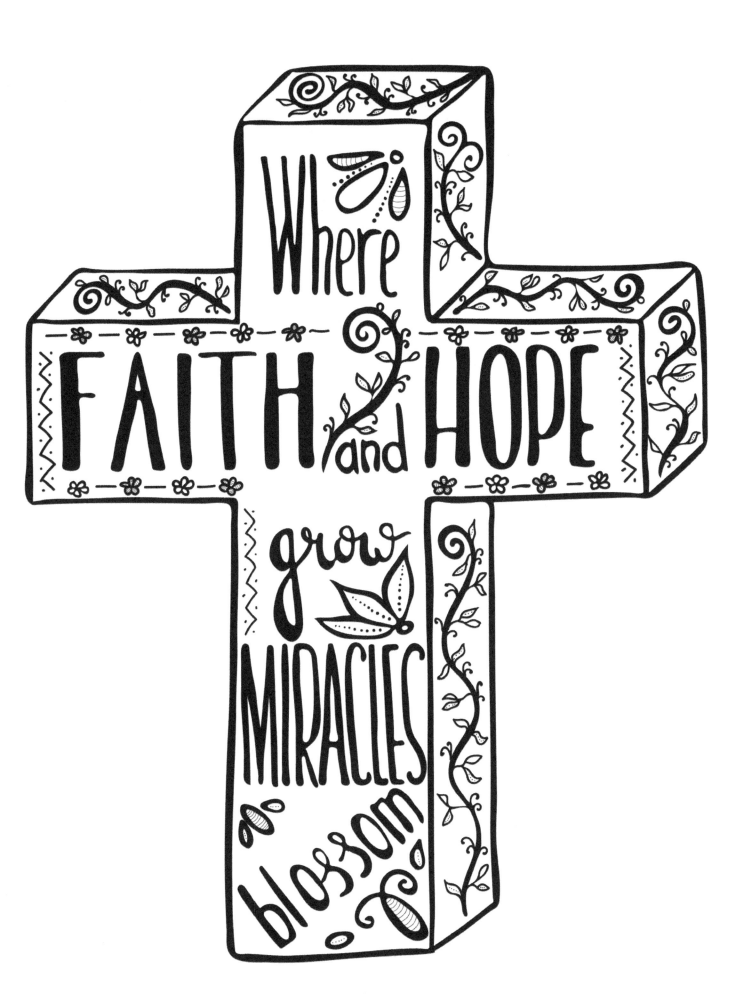

See the birds
of the sky,
that they
don't sow,
neither do they reap,
nor gather into barns.
Your heavenly Father feeds them.
Aren't you of much more value than they?

Matthew 6: 26)

Follow me and I will make you Fishers of Men

MATTHEW 4:19

You prepare a table before me
in the presence of my enemies.
You anoint my head with oil.
My cup runs over.

Psalm 23:5

The law of the wise
is a fountain
of life,

That one may depart
from the snares
of death.
Proverbs 13:14

A word fitly spoken
is like apples of gold
in settings of silver.
Proverbs 25:11

Again, the Kingdom of Heaven is
like a treasure hidden in the field,
which a man found, and hid.
In his joy, he goes
and sells all that he has,
and buys that field.

Matthew 13, 44

I'm Fearless

Psalm 34:4

Believe in the Lord Jesus Christ and you will be saved and your house

Acts 16:31

Before
I WAS BORN
GOD Choose ME
AND CALLED ME BY
HIS Marvelous GRACE
- GALATIANS 1:15 -

Look to the LORD
and his strength;
seek his face always.
1 Chronicles 16:11

Made in the USA
Las Vegas, NV
22 September 2021